A Windy Day
with Annie

Written by Michelle Fattig
Pictures by Josh Fattig

This book is dedicated
to my wonderful husband,
amazing children, and
our family.

Fattig, Michelle. A Windy Day with Annie / Michelle Fattig ; Illustrated
by Josh Fattig.

SUMMARY: In her own words, a young girl describes living with
Attention Deficit Disorder and daydreaming.

ISBN 978-0-9795805-0-5(pbk) 108 p.

Manufactured in the United States of America.

Michelle and Josh have attention deficit disorder and Asperger's Syndrome. They use their unique insight and experience to fight crime, battle evil, and promote world peace.

Contents

A Lovely Day To Daydream

Well hello there, I thought I was the only one here.

It's really not my fault, you know?

If it wasn't so deliciously cloudy,

delectably cold,

and simply *marvelous* outside,

I could pay attention.

But, that's just how it is, and I rather like it myself…

The weather that is, NOT this class!

The sound of the wind blowing through the trees is such an interesting thing, don't you think?

She just goes on, and on, and on… why should we have to learn about the Greek mythology stuff anyway? to learn about the Greek mythology stuff anyway?

I doubt very seriously that I'm going to run into one of these guys anytime soon.

I also doubt very seriously that I'm going to

need to know about the snake hair lady in order to get a decent job or even that all of this learning will find me great friends!

Sorry, what's that?

You say I look familiar?
Hmmm...
I get that a lot.
It could be the hair, or the eyes.
Maybe it's the fact that I am so completely ORDINARY!
Maybe it is also the fact that there is absolutely nothing interesting or exciting about me!

It could be that I am completely boring, boring, boring, boring with utterly no pizzazz at all.

What?

Overly dramatic you say?

Hmm...I get that a lot too.

Will you just look at that!

Ten minutes…ten long, long, long, long minutes.

Maybe, if I tried really hard, I could listen and learn a bit.

Oh, but gee look, the wind is picking up.

I just love when the wind picks up!

Hey…

What are YOU doing here?

It's the weather isn't it?

School can be very boring.

I KNOW.

I *KNOW*!

But, there is some cool stuff too.

Like have you ever just been sitting there, and out of the blue…*BAM!*

It's like a thought grabs hold of your brain and just won't let go?

No?

Hmm…
Did you have to dissect frogs in Science class?

When we dissected frogs in science class, the teacher put boys and girls together as a team.

I guess the teacher thought that if the girl was too grossed out, the boy could do the dirty deed!

Well for some reason, they stuck me with Jason.

Let's just say it wasn't
ME who ran out of the room
with a hand over my mouth!

Hoo hoo!

Did he look green around
the gills!

Run, run, *run* he did, right
to the boys' room if you know
what I mean!

Guess Mr. Maringetti was right to put us together.

After all, it was me who taught Mr. Maringetti how to fillet a fish!

No really.

I *did!*

We were supposed to be dissecting these yucky smelling perch one day, but instead I showed Mr. Maringetti how to clean them!

I guess sometimes the teacher has a thing or two to learn too.

Two, to, too…

See what I did there?

When I was younger, and my friend Camille came over to play, I would talk her into going fishing with me at our little pond.

We had trout that were so dumb; they would swallow a plain hook, with no bait or anything!

Can you believe that?

You do know what a trout is, don't you?

It's a very, very, very pretty fish.

It's almost a shame to catch them.

Hmmm…

*Any*way…

My *favorite* thing to do, was to clean the fish right in front of Camille, and then watch her run, run, *RUN* away!

*Any*way…

I'm above all of that now, of course.

I would *never* stoop to such machinations.

Cool word huh?

I found it the other day.

By found it, I don't mean it was lost; it's just that I stumbled upon it and have now claimed it as my own!

I like to claim the big words.

Words are pretty neat.

My friends think that's weird.

But how weird can it be?

M-A-C-H-I-N-A-T-I-O-N-S

And Time Flies

Man, oh man, oh *man*!
STILL more than nine
minutes to go!

I wonder if they are serving malts today with lunch.

I think it's hamburger day, which I normally like, don't get me wrong, but it's the pickles that get me.

Are normal pickles *supposed* to be *THAT* rubbery?

Do you think that they are actually slipping something in on us, trying to pretend that it's an everyday, never-mind-me pickle, when *REALLY* it could be some kind of 'smart-pill' or 'pay-attention-to-the-teacher pill?'

Hmm…

I wonder if there is a way to look that up?

Hey!

I forgot to tell you…

I'm Morgan Maryanne Marlena MacIntosh.

Not really…

I'd *like* to be!

I've heard that when you are a grown up you can change your name.

Change it to anything you want!

Can you imagine?

Why, I could think of dozens of names that are brilliant, magnificent, and *marvelous!*

Maybe I could change my name every year, maybe for my birthday.

Maybe even on my *HALF-*birthday!

Hmm…

I wonder if the telephone company would send out new books for me every time I changed my name.
Oh no.
What if they wouldn't?

What if no matter what, the books would only come out once a year?

What if no one could find me?

Guess this may take some more thought…

Morgan Maryanne Marlena MacIntosh Marrissa Melanie Mia
Michelle ...

Did you ever run for student council?

I thought about it.

I even kind of came up with a neat slogan.

I thought I'd trace this pig-shaped cutting board my mom has and say something like, "Don't be a fat pig, vote for me!"

It doesn't seem to rhyme does it?

Guess that's why I didn't run.

It would be interesting to see if anyone would vote for me, *JUST* so they wouldn't be a fat pig!

Hee *Hee.*

Now THAT'S some of that peer pressure stuff my mom is always talking about.

Does your mom ever bug
you about stuff?

I don't mean *real* stuff, like cleaning your room or washing the dishes.

I'm pretty sure there is a law that says parents *HAVE* to bug you about *THAT* stuff.

I mean weird stuff, like 'why don't you comb your hair better,' or, 'why do you have to wear the only wrinkled clothes in your drawer?'

My mom really seems to be *overly* invested in the state of my wrinkles or no-wrinkles.

Don't tell her, but sometimes I push my shirts WAY to the back of my drawer on purpose, so it has a nice wrinkly-lived-in-look.

My best friend, Gwen, is sitting over there.

No, not over there, she is over there.

She has the green shirt with that weird bird thing on the front.

She didn't used to be my best friend.

She used to be this really annoying girl I went to school with, who lived JUST near enough, that my mom made me invite her over.

I really didn't want to have her over, but when the mom announces, the kid does.

You know what I mean?

I *used* to do things like make her sleep on the mattress we keep behind the couch, for those emergency sleepovers that just seem to happen, kind of situations.

You can never be too prepared you know.

Maybe I picked that up from my brother when he was in the Boy Scouts.

A Brownie or a
Boy Scout

I always wanted to be in
the Boy Scouts, but my mom
wouldn't let me.

She made some excuse about them not letting girls in.

As *if!*

Did she really think I'd fall for *THAT* one?

She tried to appease me with Brownies.

No, not the *dessert* brownies, I mean the *BROWNIES* brownies.

You know, those little girls, who wear little brown outfits, and sell cookies.

At least I *think* they sell cookies.

And at least I *think* they wear brown uniforms.

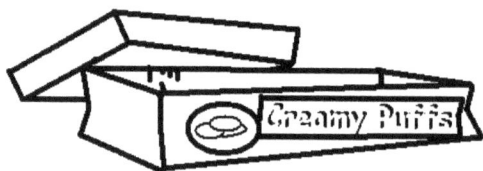

It would make *sense* that "Brownies" would wear brown, and sell cookies, wouldn't it?

Anyhoo…

It's the same mattress *I* had to sleep on when *she* broke my foot.

Yeah, she really did!

Well, SHE won't ADMIT that she did, but she *did*!

I was, graciously of course, pulling out the old mattress behind the couch, used for emergency sleepover situations, and *SHE* decided to *HELP*.

I don't mean help in a *good* way that is actually *helpful*, but more in a "helpful way" that actually *pulls* the sheet *free* from the mattress, and temporarily *over* your *head,* so you can't see where you are going, and you step off of the couch into air, and end up landing on your foot so it snaps in two, kind of way.

Did you catch the subtle difference there?

She didn't become my best friend, or even a friend that I could tolerate and not want to smack a bit, until much later on.

I used the broken foot to avoid having to see her or invite her over for some time, but eventually the mom figured out my tactics, and I was, once again, forced to play with her.

Actually, for a while, we were forced to RIDE together too.

Imagine!

Did I mention that I live
on a farm?

Two Minutes to Go

I live on a farm.

It is a small farm.

It's not really a *farm*, I guess, but more of a really, really, *really* large yard.

It's really *bigger* than a really, really, really large yard, but we don't really raise anything, so it can't be called a farm can it?

Well, I guess we *do* have ducks, which I guess TECHNICALLY means we are "raising them," in that they are actually *living* and getting *older* with us.

And we do have a *dog*, so I guess *technically* we are "raising" him too.

So… I guess it *is* a farm, just not a very *big* farm!

Hmm…
I wonder if I can look that up too?

I actually broke my cast, after I broke my foot, while lying on that same mattress we keep behind the couch, for those emergency sleepovers, that 'just-seem-to-happen,' kind of situations.

Can you believe *that?*

I used to have bunk beds.

Which really didn't make a whole lot of sense, because our ceilings are really low.

I mean our ceilings are really, *really* low!

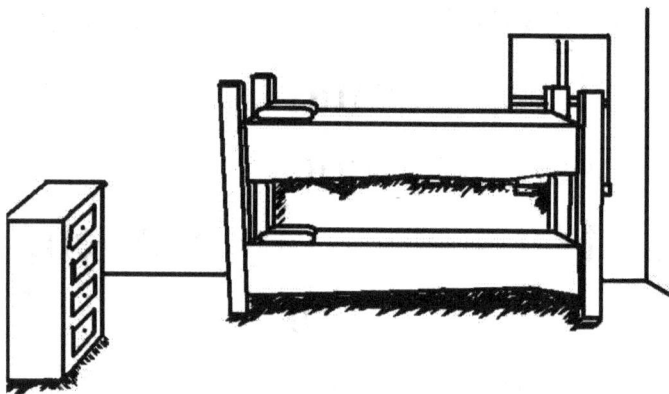

I mean, like when I jump, I can actually touch the ceiling, and sometimes when I used to run and jump into my bunk bed…well more like run and throw a leg up on the dresser and swing into my bunk bed, I would get a little carried away, and um, hmm, I think I forgot what I was saying.

That happens you know.

You are cruising along, chatting it up, and BAM!

The thought is gone.

Hey look!

Two minutes to count down!

Let's grab some of those rubbery pickle-like-pay-attention-pill things and have lunch!

Uh oh.

Mrs. Sleepotts is looking over here.

Guess maybe the weather got me again.

Really, I swear, it's not my fault.

Oh dear.

Stay in you say?

Need to talk with me about my report?

Ah, hmm, it's probably in my locker.

May I go look?

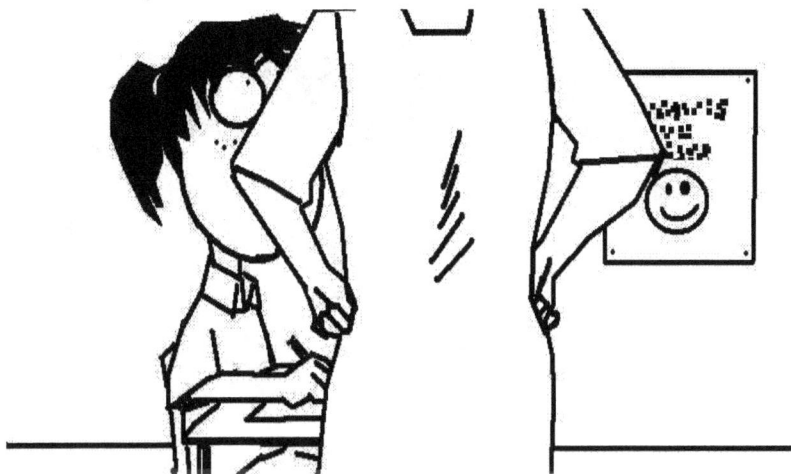

You'd best go on without me, because this could take awhile.

Dodge Ball

You're back!

We have PE now.

You know…

Physical Education, Phys Ed, the PhEdmeister.

No, I just made *that* one up.

I really like PE, except that we have to change our shoes.

I'm not above changing my shoes mind you; it's more the smelling of Tommy's feet that bothers me!

They kind of smell like a combination of old socks and really, really, REALLY, bad cheese.

Not the stuff that you forgot in the fridge, and it turned colors and kind of smells bad, kind of cheese.

I mean that really, really, REALLY fancy stuff my mom buys when *important* people not just us are coming over kind of cheese.

You know?

Tommy is a funny guy.

He always picks me first when we play scooter football in PE.

The teacher gives extra points if a girl catches the ball, so Tommy figures we are a shoe in to win every time.

Tommy says that I can go pro some day if they make a

professional scooter football league.

Hmm…

Do you think professional scooter football players would make much?

Think they might put me on a cereal box or put me in the Olympics?

I bet my mom would let me wear my perfectly-worn-in-wrinkled clothes, if I made

it to the Olympics as a scooter
football player.

Maybe not.

I like scooter football a lot, but it is not my 'all-time-favorite, I'd pick it every time if I had the choice,' kind of 'like a lot.'

No, I save THAT kind of 'like a lot' for *dodge ball!*

Dodge ball is the all time greatest PE game EVER!

I mean, you get to throw things at people and run around like crazy, and not get yelled at by an adult!

What could be better I ask you?

Well…

Except when, in the good old days, we could still jump on the trampoline.

Now trampolines were the greatest!

We could jump and do flips and bounce around.

Then, someone said we could break our necks or something, and they stole all our fun!

They try to pawn these little itty, *itty,* bitty trampolines off on us, but give me a break!

I forgot about mentioning the fun of parachute day!

Parachute day rocks, rocks, *ROCKS!*

You know parachute day don't you?

Parachute day, is when you all get around the parachute and lift it up, up, *UP* in the air, and then pull it down real hard, so it sort of billows like a cloud, or really fluffy cotton candy!

We almost lost parachute day too.

When Tommy and Kim decided to run under at the same time, well they didn't really decide to do it at the same time, they just sort of did it at the same time.

Anyhoo…

Tommy and Kim ran under at the same time and

bonked heads and Tommy had to go to the hospital.

Kim had to go to the nurse for ice.

After that, they *almost* took parachute day away because, apparently, unsafe parachute play can cause concussions!

Bet they don't put *that* warning on the parachute box!

What Mr. Smith?

Oh, yes sorry.

I'm coming right now.

Oh man!

Archery day?

Woo hoo!

I forgot how great archery day is!

Maybe I'll see you later. I'm coming Mr. Smith!

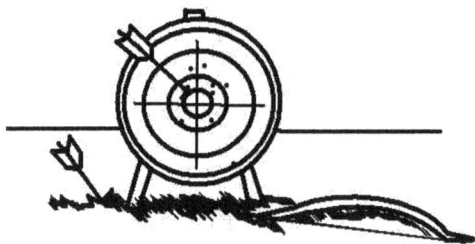

Best Friend?
I Think Not!

You are still here I see.

Do you want to walk with me to class?

Remember when I showed you my best friend, who didn't used to be my best friend, who was wearing the green shirt with that weird bird thing on the front?

Did I tell you about the slumber party at her cousin's house where she ate talcum powder by accident?

Hoo hoo…

It was one of the funniest moments EVER!

Since we live on a farm.

Well.. sort of a farm.

Well.. you know.

We don't have many close neighbors.

Since we don't have many close neighbors, my mom says she is not driving to Timbuktu and back.

That is a place, which is far, far, *far* away!

Really.

It is.

I looked it up!

Anyhoo…

Any kids, who lived anywhere close to us, and went to our school, were considered prime friend potential, at least by *my* mom anyway!

Well, if you remember, Gwen and I were not very fond of each other to begin with.

That was, of course, a long, long, LONG time ago.

Now we are, of course, the best, best, *BEST* of friends.

Well, Gwen's cousin was my friend.

A friend I LIKED, *NOT* one that my mom picked so she didn't have to drive to Timbuktu.

She lives on a farm too.

A real farm though, not a small. sort-of-like-a-farm, like we live on.

Her dad drives big, big, *BIG* tractors and has giant cows and everything!

Her name is Trista, and she also ate a spider at the

party, but that is a whole other story!

We were, all three of us, pretending to have fun.

Because, after all, Gwen was still the kind of "pretend friend that my mom forced on me and I kind of wanted to smack a bit," kind of friend at that time.

It was somebody's bright idea; probably mine, because I usually had the bright ideas!

Don't tell them I said so.

Anyhoo…

It was somebody's bright idea to make up skits.

Do you know what a skit is?

You know, like mini plays sort of.

You and your friends make up funny characters and

lines and dance around to make your friends laugh.

Even if they are the kind of, "pretend friend that my mom forced on me and I kind of wanted to smack a bit," kind.

Well…

I was brilliant and had them rolling and laughing and holding their stomachs.

At least that is the way I remember it.

So Gwen, who I also suspect wanted to smack me a bit, was determined to be funnier, brighter, and more, more, *MORE* entertaining.

Gwen got this funny old hat and used a funny old gray wig and some funny old pants.

She humped over and walked around like an old man.

We thought this was VERY funny indeed.

That made Gwen very happy because she wanted to be funny, funny, *funnier* than me!

Gwen started to dance around and kick up her knees.

We laughed harder.

Gwen talked and sang in an old man voice.

We laughed harder yet!

Gwen picked up an old talcum powder bottle and pretended it was her, or "his" if you like, drink.

We laughed.

Gwen tipped it up to drink……..

And what do you know……..

The talcum powder bottle was *OPEN*.

The talcum powder bottle was *FULL*.

The talcum powder must not have tasted very good judging by the look on Gwen's face!

Gwen's eyes opened wide. Her mouth fell open.

Her white, powder covered tongue shot out of her mouth like some kind of strange fuzzy, white, creature.

Gwen just stood there
like that for what seemed like
a long, long, LONG time!

I couldn't believe what I was seeing.

Now remember, I was none too fond of Gwen back then.

I started to chuckle, I
started to giggle, I started to
rumble, I started to guffaw,

I started to laugh so hard my eyes started to water.

Gwen suddenly bolted for
the door!

Water, she needed water to rinse out her mouth!

She ran to the bathroom, but Trista's mom was taking a bath!

Gwen ran up the long dark hallway wiping at her tongue.

Gwen ran down the long dark hallway wiping at her tongue.

Gwen, finally, dashed down, down, *DOWN* the staircase, through the dining room, across the hallway, over the dog sleeping on the floor, into the kitchen.

She stuck her head under the faucet, plastering her hair smack to her face.

When Gwen stood up, her gray wig was dripping and falling down into her eyes.

Her hat had fallen off into the sink, where Trista's mom had been peeling potatoes.

When she lifted it back out and put it on her head, she had potato peelings falling around her ears.

In the mad dash, her pants had ended up down around her ankles.

The talcum powder appeared in watery, white, streaks all down her face and the front of her shirt.

Now if you recall.

Gwen had been trying to out-funny me.

You know what?

I think she did it!

Well.

Here we are.

Maybe I'll see you later?

Oh yeah, I forgot to tell you… my name is Victoria, the Vic-ster, Victorious Victoria. Vics, VickAAAY, Toria the Vic!

But my friends call me Annie.

See ya!

We hope you have enjoyed this book with Annie. For more Annie Books Series, see www.anniebooks.com

-Michelle, Josh, and Victoria Lilianne

www.ingramcontent.com/pod-product-compliance
Lightning Source LLC
Chambersburg PA
CBHW050532280326
41933CB00011B/1552

Praise for the New Approach:

"*Chalyce's protocol is a lifestyle change for better health. Nature is a powerful medicine. More people need to learn the power of natural healing.*"
–Alais Howard Reta

"*Your oils changed my life. I was bedridden, unable to even keep a cracker down. I went from doctor to doctor taking prescription after prescription, enduring horrible side effects. I was on the verge of having surgery and giving up on life. One day I came across your page and started reading about your oils and the lifestyle changes suggested. It's been about four months and I am amazed at how much I have healed. I have more energy and am actually eating solid food, something I never thought I could do again!*"
–Cindy Cook

"*I have been using the oils religiously for two weeks now and what a difference. I am eating again and able to get up and do things and be active. I am so thankful.*"
–Amy Sneddon

"*I am telling you this protocol will help your quality of life! You just have to be patient and you have to be conscious of when and what you eat.*"
–Carol Ulmer

"*The essential oils and protocols work the best to manage my symptoms. I haven't gotten to a place where food is my friend yet, but without the oils, sauerkraut juice and kefir, I wouldn't be eating at all. For that I am blessed. For anyone struggling with impaired digestion or constipation issues, there is help.*"
–Cari Oppen

ISBN: 978-0-692-77024-5
Healing GP Naturally
807 Lucille Ave
Nokomis, FL 34275

Developmental Editor:
Janice Brewster, www.creativegirlfriendspress.com

Cover and Book Designer:
Sean Keenan, sean@keenankreative.com

Disclaimer
THIS BOOK IS NOT INTENDED FOR THE PURPOSE OF PROVIDING MEDICAL ADVICE
All information, content and material in this book is for informational purposes only and is not intended to serve as a substitute for the consultation, diagnosis and/or medical treatment of a qualified physician or healthcare provider. The authors of this book, and the publisher, specifically disclaim all responsibility for any liability, loss or risk, personal or otherwise, which is incurred as a consequence, directly or indirectly, of the use and application of any of the material shared.